GET MOTIVATED FOR SUCCESS IN YOUR BUSINESS!

GET MOTIVATED FOR SUCCESS IN YOUR BUSINESS!

A MOTIVATIONAL BUSINESS QUOTE FOR EVERY MORNING AND EVERY AFTERNOON OF EVERY DAY OF THE YEAR

JESSICA ORBEN

CruGuru

GET MOTIVATED FOR SUCCESS IN YOUR BUSINESS!

Copyright © 2008 by Jessica Orben

ISBN: 978-1-920265-18-2

Published in 2008 by CruGuru

www.cruguru.com

Johannesburg, South Africa

Foreword

I have always referred to quotes about motivation, leadership, business management, inspiration, etc. to keep me motivated when running my business. These quotes have a way to get stuck into my head and enthuse me when times get tough.

In *"Get Motivated for Success in Your Business!"* I have provided a powerful motivational business quote for every morning and every afternoon of every day of the year. I hope they inspire you in the same positive way as they did for me!

The Author

2008

Table of Contents

JANUARY

AM:

Every great and commanding movement in the annals of the world is a triumph of enthusiasm.

Ralph Waldo Emerson

PM:

Natural ability without education has more often raised a man to glory and virtue than education without natural ability.

Cicero

AM:

Don't blame the marketing department. The buck stops with the chief executive.

John D. Rockefeller

PM:

Advertising is the life of trade.

Calvin Coolidge

JANUARY 3

AM:

Optimism is essential to achieve-ment and it is also the founda-tion of courage and true progress.

Nicholas M. Butler

PM:

Buy land. They ain't making any more of the stuff.

Will Rogers

JANUARY 4

AM:

A truly good book teaches me better than to read it. I must soon lay it down, and commence living on its hint. What I began by reading, I must finish by acting.

Henry David Thoreau

PM:

We learn wisdom from failure much more than from success. We often discover what will do, by finding out what will not do; and probably he who never made a mistake never made a discovery.

Samuel Smiles

JANUARY 5

AM:

If everyone is thinking alike, then somebody isn't thinking.

George S. Patton

PM:

No person will make a great business who wants to do it all himself or get all the credit.

Andrew Carnegie

JANUARY 6

AM:

The best executive is the one who has sense enough to pick good men to do what he wants done, and self-restraint to keep from meddling with them while they do it.

Theodore Roosevelt

PM:

A man's as miserable as he thinks he is.

Lucius Annaeus Seneca

JANUARY 7

AM:

Experience teaches us that it is much easier to prevent an enemy from posting themselves than it is to dislodge them after they have got possession.

George Washington

PM:

People who are unable to motivate themselves must be content with mediocrity, no matter how impressive their other talents.

Andrew Carnegie

JANUARY 8

AM:

To open a shop is easy, to keep it open is an art.

Chinese Proverb

PM:

Do not wait; the time will never be "just right." Start where you stand, and work with whatever tools you may have at your command, and better tools will be found as you go along.

George Herbert

JANUARY 9

AM:

Sometimes we stare so long at a door that is closing that we see too late the one that is open.

Alexander Graham Bell

PM:

Do the thing you fear most and the death of fear is certain.

Mark Twain

JANUARY 10

AM:

When dealing with people, let us remember that we are not dealing with creatures of logic. We are dealing with creatures of emotion, creatures bursting with prejudice and motivated by pride and vanity

Dale Carnegie

PM:

I never did a day's work in my life. It was all fun.

Thomas Edison

JANUARY 11

AM:

Unless a man undertakes more than he possibly can do, he will never do all that he can.

Henry Drummond

PM:

I find the great thing in this world is not so much where we stand, as in what direction we are moving.

Oliver Wendell Holmes, Sr.

JANUARY 12

AM:

You're never beaten until you admit it.

George S. Patton

PM:

The game of life is a game of boomerangs. Our thoughts, deeds and words return to us sooner or later with astounding accuracy.

Florence Scovel Shinn

JANUARY 13

AM:

We must walk consciously only part way toward our goal, and then leap in the dark to our success.

Henry David Thoreau

PM:

Persist and persevere, and you will find most things that are attainable, possible.

Lord Chesterfield

JANUARY 14

AM:

Success bases our worth on a comparison with others. Excellence gauges our value by measuring us against our own potential.

Dale Carnegie

PM:

No one can make you feel inferior without your consent.

Eleanor Roosevelt

JANUARY 15

AM:

Prosperity is only an instrument to be used, not a deity to be worshipped.

Calvin Coolidge

PM:

To me faith means not worrying.

John Dewey

JANUARY 16

AM:

Tell me and I forget. Teach me and I remember. Involve me and I learn.

Benjamin Franklin

PM:

By failing to prepare, you are preparing to fail.

Benjamin Franklin

JANUARY 17

AM:

Be wary of the man who urges an action in which he himself incurs no risk.

Lucius Annaeus Seneca

PM:

Every right implies a responsibility; Every opportunity, an obligation, Every possession, a duty.

John D. Rockefeller

JANUARY 18

AM:

A somebody was once a nobody who wanted to and did.

John Burroughs

PM:

Only that day dawns to which we are awake.

Henry David Thoreau

JANUARY 19

AM:

The way to get things done is not to mind who gets the credit for doing them.

Benjamin Jowet

PM:

Genius is talent set on fire by courage.

Henry van Dyke

JANUARY 20

AM:

All successful employers are stalking men who will do the unusual, men who think, men who attract attention by performing more than is expected of them.

Charles M. Schwab

PM:

Good leadership consists of showing average people how to do the work of superior people.

John D. Rockefeller

JANUARY 21

AM:

Any fool can criticize, condemn and complain and most fools do.

Benjamin Franklin

PM:

Ordinary riches can be stolen; real riches cannot. In your soul are infinitely precious things that cannot be taken from you.

Oscar Wilde

JANUARY 22

AM:

Heroism is not only in the man, but in the occasion.

Calvin Coolidge

PM:

People only see what they are prepared to see. Ralph

Waldo Emerson

JANUARY 23

AM:

There is hardly anything in the world that some man cannot make a little worse, and sell a little cheaper.

John Ruskin

PM:

Do your duty in all things. You cannot do more, you should never wish to do less.

Robert E. Lee

JANUARY 24

AM:

Life has taught me to think, but thinking has not taught me to live.

Alexander Herzen

PM:

Our greatest glory consists not in never failing, but in rising every time we fall.

Oliver Goldsmith

JANUARY 25

AM:

Every man of courage is a man of his word.

Pierre Corneille

PM:

Think you can, think you can't; either way you'll be right.

Henry Ford

JANUARY 26

AM:

I always tried to turn every disaster into an opportunity.

John D. Rockefeller

PM:

Compassion will cure more sins than condemnation.

Henry Ward Beecher

JANUARY 27

AM:

Out of difficulties grow miracles.

Jean De La Bruyere

PM:

A wise man is he who does not grieve for the things which he has not, but rejoices for those which he has.

Epictetus

JANUARY 28

AM:

The battle of life is, in most cases, fought uphill; and to win it without a struggle were perhaps to win it without honor. If there were no difficulties there would be no success; if there were nothing to struggle for, there would be nothing to be achieved.

Samuel Smiles

PM:

Your net worth to the world is usually determined by what remains after your bad habits are subtracted from your good ones.

Benjamin Franklin

JANUARY 29

AM:

Exellence is available to all living beings, but accepted by few.

Dale Carnegie

PM:

To succeed, jump as quickly at opportunities as you do at conclusions.

Benjamin Franklin

JANUARY 30

AM:

The most effective way to do it, is to do it.

Amelia Earhart

PM:

There is this difference between happiness and wisdom, that he that thinks himself the happiest man, really is so; but he who thinks himself the wisest, is generally the greatest fool.

C.C. Colton

JANUARY 31

AM:

It is better to offer no excuse than a bad one.

George Washington

PM:

Whosoever desires constant success must change his conduct with the times.

Niccolo Machiavelli

FEBRUARY

AM:

What you are will show in what you do.

Thomas Edison

PM:

I believe in the dignity of labor, whether with head or hand; that the world owes no man a living but that it owes every man an opportunity to make a living.

John D. Rockefeller

AM:

Nothing will ever be attempted, if all possible objections must first be overcome.

Samuel Johnson

PM:

Encouragement is a necessary part of supervision.

Thomas J. Watson

FEBRUARY 3

AM:

The most wasted of all days is that during which one has not laughed.

Sebastian Chamfort

PM:

One man gives freely, yet gains even more; another withholds unduly, but comes to poverty.

Proverbs 11:24

FEBRUARY 4

AM:

All that we achieve or fail to achieve is the direct result of our thoughts.

James Allen

PM:

You cannot help men permanently by doing for them what they could and should do for themselves.

Abraham Lincoln

FEBRUARY 5

AM:

Genius may have its limitations, but stupidity is not thus handi-capped.

Elbert Hubbard

PM:

We learn by doing.

Aristotle

FEBRUARY 6

AM:

Duty is not collective; it is personal.

Calvin Coolidge

PM:

Difficulties strengthen the mind, as labor does the body.

Lucius Annaeus Seneca

FEBRUARY 7

AM:

Adversity is the foundation of virtue.

Japanese Proverb

PM:

Even after a bad harvest there must be sowing.

Lucius Annaeus Seneca

FEBRUARY 8

AM:

To teach is to learn.

Japanese Proverb

PM:

Nothing in this world can take the place of persistence. Talent will not; nothing is more common than unsuccessful people with talent. Genius will not; unrewarded genius is almost a proverb.

Calvin Coolidge

FEBRUARY 9

AM:

How wonderful it is to say the right thing at the right time. A good man thinks before he speaks; the evil man pours out his evil words without a thought.

Proverbs 15:23,28

PM:

The beginning of a habit is like an invisible thread, but every time we repeat the act we strengthen the strand, add to it another filament, until it becomes a great cable and binds us irrevocably through thought and act.

Orison Swett Marden

FEBRUARY 10

AM:

Man cannot aspire if he looked down; if he rise, he must look up.

Samuel Smiles

PM:

There are many paths to the top of the mountain, but the view is always the same.

Chinese Proverb

FEBRUARY 11

AM:

Behind an able man there are always other able men.

Chinese Proverb

PM:

Doing easily what others find difficult is talent; doing what is impossible for talent is genius.

Henri Frederic Amiel

FEBRUARY 12

AM:

In any moment of decision, the best thing you can do is the right thing. The worst thing you can do is nothing.

Theodore Roosevelt

PM:

Who dares to teach must never cease to learn.

John Cotton Dana

FEBRUARY 13

AM:

One man with courage makes a majority.

Andrew Jackson

PM:

A wise man listens to advice.

Proverbs 12:15

FEBRUARY 14

AM:

The worst sorrows in life are not in its losses and misfortunes, but its fears.

A. C. Benson

PM:

Some things in the world are far more important than wealth; one of them is the ability to enjoy simple things.

Dale Carnegie

FEBRUARY 15

AM:

There is nothing as easy as denouncing. It doesn't take much to see that something is wrong, but it does take some eyesight to see what will put it right again.

Will Rogers

PM:

I cannot teach anybody anything, I can only make them think.

Socrates

FEBRUARY 16

AM:

I do not think that there is any other quality so essential to success of any kind as the quality of perseverance. It overcomes almost everything, even nature.

John D. Rockefeller

PM:

There is no personal charm so great as the charm of a cheerful temperament.

Henry van Dyke

FEBRUARY 17

AM:

Wise men don't need advice. Fools won't take it.

Benjamin Franklin

PM:

Every advantage in the past is judged in the light of the final issue.

Demosthenes

FEBRUARY 18

AM:

Common sense is calculation applied to life.

Henri Frederic Amiel

PM:

You will never stub a toe standing still. The faster you go, the more chance there is of stubbing your toe, but the more chance you have of getting somewhere.

Charles F. Kettering

FEBRUARY 19

AM:

We know what happens to people who stay in the middle of the road. They get run over.

Ambrose Bierce

PM:

The important thing is this: To be able at any moment to sacrifice what we are for what we could become.

Charles du Bos

FEBRUARY 20

AM:

I will pay more for the ability to deal with people than any other ability under the sun.

John D. Rockefeller

PM:

Idleness is only the refuge of weak minds.

Lord Chesterfield

FEBRUARY 21

AM:

Do the right thing. It will gratify some people and astonish the rest.

Mark Twain

PM:

I am a great believer in luck, and I find the harder I work the more I have of it.

Stephen Leacock

FEBRUARY 22

AM:

A failure establishes only this; that our determination to succeed was not strong enough.

John Christian Bovee

PM:

Work is not man's punishment. It is his reward and his strength and his pleasure.

George Sand

FEBRUARY 23

AM:

He that composes himself is wiser than he that composes a book.

Benjamin Franklin

PM:

There is no such thing as luck. It's a fancy name for being always at our duty, and so sure to be ready when good time comes.

Robert Bulwer-Lytton

FEBRUARY 24

AM:

He was a man, he always performed his promises.

Zebulon Pike

PM:

Our greatest weakness lies in giving up. The most certain way to succeed is to always try just one more time.

Thomas Edison

FEBRUARY 25

AM:

I know of nothing more despicable and pathetic than a man who devotes all the hours of the waking day to the making of money for money's sake.

John D. Rockefeller

PM:

The mind that is anxious about the future is miserable.

Lucius Annaeus Seneca

FEBRUARY 26

AM:

He who never made a mistake, never made a discovery.

Samuel Smiles

PM:

Do what you can, with what you have, where you are.

Theodore Roosevelt

FEBRUARY 27

AM:

Advice is seldom welcome, and those who need it most like it the least.

Samuel Johnson

PM:

If passion drives you, let reason hold the reins.

Benjamin Franklin

FEBRUARY 28

AM:

Obstacles are those frightful things you see when you take your eyes off your goal.

Henry Ford

PM:

If you want to succeed you should strike out on new paths, rather than travel the worn paths of accepted success.

John D. Rockefeller

FEBRUARY 29

AM:

The world hates change, yet it is the only thing that has brought progress.

Charles F. Kettering

PM:

Whether you think that you can, or that you can't, you are usually right.

Henry Ford

MARCH

AM:

Wisdom is the power to put our time and our knowledge to the proper use.

Thomas J. Watson

PM:

Wisdom and understanding can only become the possession of individual men by travelling the old road of observation, attention, perseverance, and industry.

Samuel Smiles

AM:

Character is the result of two things: mental attitude and the way we spend our time.

Elbert Hubbard

PM:

Experience is the name everyone gives to their mistakes.

Oscar Wilde

MARCH 3

AM:

You have not lived today successfully unless you've done something for someone who can never repay you.

John Bunyan

PM:

Every great advance in science has issued from a new audacity of imagination.

John Dewey

MARCH 4

AM:

For anything worth having one must pay the price; and the price is always work, patience, love, self-sacrifice - no paper currency, no promises to pay, but the gold of real service.

John Burroughs

PM:

I am indeed rich, since my income is superior to my expenses, and my expense is equal to my wishes.

Edward Gibbon

MARCH 5

AM:

Every blunder behind us is giving a cheer for us, and only for those who were willing to fail are the dangers and splendors of life.

Carl Sandburg

PM:

Far better is it to dare mighty things, to win glorious triumphs, even though checkered by failure... than to rank with those poor spirits who neither enjoy nor suffer much, because they live in a grey twilight that knows not victory nor defeat.

Theodore Roosevelt

MARCH 6

AM:

Failure is instructive. The person who really thinks learns quite as much from his failures as from his successes.

John Dewey

PM:

It's good to have money and the things that money can buy, but it's good, too, to check once in a while and make sure that you haven't lost things that money can't buy.

George Horace Lorimer

MARCH 7

AM:

The first and worst of all frauds is to cheat oneself.

Gamaliel Bailey

PM:

Act like you expect to get into the end zone.

Christopher Morley

MARCH 8

AM:

What we do belongs to what we are; and what we are is what becomes of us.

Henry van Dyke

PM:

What you possess in the world will be found at the day of your death to belong to someone else. But what you are will be yours forever.

Henry van Dyke

MARCH 9

AM:

The wise man saves for the future, but the foolish man spends whatever he gets.

Proverbs 21:20

PM:

Man's mind, once stretched by a new idea, never regains its original dimensions.

Oliver Wendell Holmes, Sr.

MARCH 10

AM:

Never think that you're not good enough yourself. A man should never think that. People will take you very much at your own reckoning.

Anthony Trollope

PM:

A generous man will prosper; he who refreshes others will himself be refreshed.

Proverbs 11:25

MARCH 11

AM:

Tricks and treachery are the practice of fools that don't have brains enough to be honest.

Benjamin Franklin

PM:

Dreams are the touchstones of our character.

Henry David Thoreau

MARCH 12

AM:

Lack of money is the root of all evil.

George Bernard Shaw

PM:

It's a fine thing to rise above pride, but you must have pride in order to do so.

Georges Bernanos

MARCH 13

AM:

The past, the present and the future are really one: they are today.

Harriet Beecher Stowe

PM:

Well done is better than well said.

Benjamin Franklin

MARCH 14

AM:

Mind unemployed is mind unenjoyed.

John Christian Bovee

PM:

You have to have your heart in the business and the business in your heart.

Thomas J. Watson

MARCH 15

AM:

We improve ourselves by victories over ourselves. There must be contest, and we must win.

Edward Gibbon

PM:

You will never do anything in this world without courage. It is the greatest quality of the mind next to honor.

Aristotle

MARCH 16

AM:

Without some goals and some efforts to reach it, no man can live.

John Dewey

PM:

To put the world right in order, we must first put the nation in order; to put the nation in order, we must first put the family in order; to put the family in order, we must first cultivate our personal life; we must first set our hearts right.

Confucius

MARCH 17

AM:

Our life is frittered away by detail... simplify, simplify.

Henry David Thoreau

PM:

Golf without bunkers and hazards would be tame and monotonous. So would life.

B. C. Forbes

MARCH 18

AM:

The best thing about the future is that it comes one day at a time.

Abraham Lincoln

PM:

Opportunity is missed by most people because it is dressed in overalls and looks like work.

Thomas Edison

MARCH 19

AM:

Our greatest weakness lies in giving up. The most certain way to succeed is always to try just one more time.

Thomas Edison

PM:

The beginning is the most important part of the work.

Plato

MARCH 20

AM:

A great pleasure in life is doing what people say you cannot do.

Walter Bagehot

PM:

Few things can help an individual more than to place responsibility on him, and to let him know that you trust him

Booker T. Washington

MARCH 21

AM:

The experience gathered from books, though often valuable, is but the nature of learning; whereas the experience gained from actual life is one of the nature of wisdom.

Samuel Smiles

PM:

As a small businessperson, you have no greater leverage than the truth.

John Greenleaf Whittier

MARCH 22

AM:

We aim above the mark to hit the mark.

Ralph Waldo Emerson

PM:

With audacity one can undertake anything, but not do everything.

Napoleon Bonaparte

MARCH 23

AM:

We work to become, not to acquire.

Elbert Hubbard

PM:

Pleasure in the job puts perfection in the work.

Aristotle

MARCH 24

AM:

No problem can be solved until it is reduced to some simple form. The changing of a vague difficulty into a specific, concrete form is a very essential element in thinking.

J.P. Morgan

PM:

A person without a sense of humor is like a wagon without springs. It's jolted by every pebble on the road.

Henry Ward Beecher

MARCH 25

AM:

Any man worth his salt will stick up for what he believes right, but it takes a slightly better man to acknowledge instantly and without reservation that he is in error.

Andrew Jackson

PM:

Never despair, but if you do, work on in despair.

Edmund Burke

MARCH 26

AM:

Towering genius disdains a beaten path. It seeks regions hitherto unexplored.

Abraham Lincoln

PM:

There is no greater joy than that of feeling oneself a creator. The triumph of life is expressed by creation.

Henri Bergson

MARCH 27

AM:

The one who adapts his policy to the times prospers, and likewise that the one whose policy clashes with the demands of the times does not.

Niccolo Machiavelli

PM:

Beware lest in your anxiety to avoid war you obtain a master.

Demosthenes

MARCH 28

AM:

The absent are always in the wrong.

English Proverb

PM:

I count him braver who overcomes his desires than him who overcomes his enemies, for the hardest victory is victory over self.

Aristotle

MARCH 29

AM:

If we did all the things we are capable of, we would literally astound ourselves.

Thomas Edison

PM:

Let no man imagine that he has no influence. Whoever he may be, and wherever he may be placed, the man who thinks becomes a light and a power.

Henry George

MARCH 30

AM:

The pressure of adversity does not affect the mind of the brave man... It is more powerful than external circumstances.

Lucius Annaeus Seneca

PM:

Men do not die from overwork. They die from dissipation and worry.

Charles Evans Hughes

MARCH 31

AM:

Character is like a tree and reputation like its shadow. The shadow is what we think of it; the tree is the real thing.

Abraham Lincoln

PM:

What kills a skunk is the publicity it gives itself.

Abraham Lincoln

APRIL

APRIL 1

AM:

Little minds attain and are subdued by misfortunes; but great minds rise above them.

Washington Irving

PM:

There is no mistake so great as the mistake of not going on.

William Blake

APRIL 2

AM:

Do not go where the path may lead, go instead where there is no path and leave a trail.

Ralph Waldo Emerson

PM:

None are so old as those who have outlived enthusiasm.

Henry David Thoreau

APRIL 3

AM:

A great thing can only be done by a great person; and they do it without effort.

John Ruskin

PM:

Genius is one percent inspiration and ninety-nine percent perspiration.

Thomas Edison

APRIL 4

AM:

The toughest thing about the power of trust is that it's very difficult to build and very easy to destroy. The essence of trust building is to emphasize the similarities between you and the customer.

Thomas J. Watson

PM:

Our truest life is when we are in dreams awake.

Henry David Thoreau

APRIL 5

AM:

A little thought and a little kindness are often worth more than a great deal of money.

John Ruskin

PM:

No one makes a revolution by himself.

George Sand

APRIL 6

AM:

Try not to become a man of success, but rather try to become a man of value.

Albert Einstein

PM:

Few men during their lifetime comes anywhere near exhausting the resources dwelling within them. There are deep wells of strength that are never used.

Richard E. Byrd

APRIL 7

AM:

He who wrestles with us strengthens our nerves and sharpens our skill. Our antagonist is our helper.

Edmund Burke

PM:

Never look back unless you are planning to go that way.

Henry David Thoreau

APRIL 8

AM:

We become wiser by adversity; prosperity destroys our appreciation of the right.

Lucius Annaeus Seneca

PM:

The man of integrity walks securely, but he who takes crooked paths will be found out.

Proverbs 10:9

APRIL 9

AM:

A man to carry on a successful business must have imagination. He must see things as in a vision, a dream of the whole thing.

Charles M. Schwab

PM:

A manager is an assistant to his men.

Thomas J. Watson

APRIL 10

AM:

The secret of happiness is something to do.

John Burroughs

PM:

We cannot do everything at once, but we can do something at once.

Calvin Coolidge

APRIL 11

AM:

The best preparation for good work tomorrow is to do good work today.

Elbert Hubbard

PM:

What we do on some great occasion will probably depend on what we already are; and what we are will be the result of previous years of self-discipline.

H.P. Liddon

APRIL 12

AM:

Far and away the best price that life offers is the chance to work hard at work worth doing.

Theodore Roosevelt

PM:

Hope is like the sun, which, as we journey toward it, casts the shadow of our burden behind us.

Samuel Smiles

APRIL 13

AM:

The confidence which we have in ourselves gives birth to much of that which we have in others.

Francois de la Rochefoucauld

PM:

To be trusted is a greater complement than to be loved.

George MacDonald

APRIL 14

AM:

From now until the end of time no one else will ever see life with my eyes, and I mean to make the best of my chance.

Christopher Morley

PM:

The more extensive a man's knowledge of what has been done, the greater will be his power of knowing what to do.

Benjamin Disraeli

APRIL 15

AM:

He is rich or poor according to what he is, not according to what he has.

Henry Ward Beecher

PM:

Not until we are lost do we begin to understand ourselves.

Henry David Thoreau

APRIL 16

AM:

There are two days in the week about which and upon which I never worry: One.. is yesterday... and the other day I do not worry about is tomorrow.

Robert J. Burdette

PM:

Thoughts lead on to purposes; purposes go forth in action; actions form habits; habits decide character; and character fixes our destiny.

Tyron Edwards

APRIL 17

AM:

The distance is nothing; it is only the first step that is difficult.

Mme. Du Deffand

PM:

Do not think of your faults, still less of other's faults; look for what is good and strong, and try to imitate it. Your faults will drop off, like dead leaves, when their time comes.

John Ruskin

APRIL 18

AM:

It is not how much one makes but to what purpose one spends.

John Ruskin

PM:

The art of being wise is knowing what to overlook.

William James

APRIL 19

AM:

A thought which does not result in an action is nothing much, and an action which does not proceed from a thought is nothing at all.

Georges Bernanos

PM:

A man who trims himself to suit everybody will soon whittle himself away.

Charles M. Schwab

APRIL 20

AM:

Courage is the greatest of all the virtues. Because if you haven't courage, you may not have an opportunity to use any of the others.

Samuel Johnson

PM:

Arriving at one goal is the starting point to another.

John Dewey

APRIL 21

AM:

Better never begin than never make an end.

George Herbert

PM:

When everything seems to be going against you, remember that the airplane takes off against the wind, not with it.

Henry Ford

APRIL 22

AM:

I have found it advisable not to give too much heed to what people say when I am trying to accomplish something of consequence. Invariably they proclaim it can't be done. I deem that the very best time to make the effort.

Calvin Coolidge

PM:

Nothing ever comes to one, that is worth having, except as a result of hard work.

Booker T. Washington

APRIL 23

AM:

It is not the employer who pays the wages. Employers only handle the money. It is the customer who pays the wages.

Henry Ford

PM:

Skill and confidence are an unconquered army.

George Herbert

APRIL 24

AM:

When a customer enters my store, forget me. He is king.

John Wanamaker

PM:

It takes as much energy to wish as it does to plan.

Eleanor Roosevelt

APRIL 25

AM:

Enthusiasm... the sustaining power of all great action.

Samuel Smiles

PM:

Every production of genius must be the production of enthusiasm.

Benjamin Disraeli

APRIL 26

AM:

Better a red face than a black heart.

Portuguese proverb

PM:

In the middle of difficulty lies opportunity.

Albert Einstein

APRIL 27

AM:

No one can arrive from being talented alone, work transforms talent into genius.

Anna Pavlova

PM:

Make the most of the best and the least of the worst.

Robert Louis Stevenson

APRIL 28

AM:

Quality is never an accident. It is always the result of intelligent effort.

John Ruskin

PM:

One man has enthusiasm for 30 minutes, another for 30 days, but it is the man who has it for 30 years who makes a success of his life.

Edward B. Butler

APRIL 29

AM:

No enterprise can exist for itself alone. It ministers to some great need, it performs some great service, not for itself, but for others; or failing therein, it ceases to be profitable and ceases to exist.

Calvin Coolidge

PM:

Knowledge without wisdom is a load of books on the back of a donkey.

Japanese Proverb

APRIL 30

AM:

Skill is the unified force of experience, intellect and passion in their operation.

John Ruskin

PM:

It is astonishing what an effort it seems to be for many people to put their brains definitely and systematically to work.

Thomas Edison

MAY

AM:

It is not the going out of port, but the coming in, that determines the success of a voyage.

Henry Ward Beecher

PM:

The most difficult thing is the decision to act, the rest is merely tenacity. The fears are paper tigers. You can do anything you decide to do. You can act to change and control your life; and the procedure, the process is its own reward.

Amelia Earhart

AM:

Nothing comes merely by thinking about it.

John Wanamaker

PM:

An intense anticipation itself transforms possibility into reality; our desires being often but precursors of the things which we are capable of performing.

Samuel Smiles

MAY 3

AM:

Persistent people begin their success where others end in failure.

Edward Eggleston

PM:

Initiative is doing the right things without being told.

Elbert Hubbard

MAY 4

AM:

Associate yourself with people of good quality, for it is better to be alone than in bad company.

Booker T. Washington

PM:

I have learned that success is to be measured not so much by the position that one has reached in life as by the obstacles which he has had to overcome while trying to succeed.

Booker T. Washington

MAY 5

AM:

Learn from your mistakes and build on your successes.

John C. Calhoun

PM:

The future belongs to those who believe in the beauty of their dreams.

Eleanor Roosevelt

MAY 6

AM:

Leaders should lead as far as they can and then vanish. Their ashes should not choke the fire they have lit.

H.G. Wells

PM:

Use what talent you possess. The woods would be very silent if no birds sang except those that sang best.

Henry van Dyke

MAY 7

AM:

You learn to know a pilot in a storm.

Lucius Annaeus Seneca

PM:

If you are planning for a year, sow rice; if you are planning for a decade, plant trees; if you are planning for a lifetime, educate people.

Chinese Proverb

MAY 8

AM:

A shady business never yields a sunny life.

B. C. Forbes

PM:

All men who have turned out worth anything have had the chief hand in their own education.

Walter Scott

MAY 9

AM:

Do you love life? Then do not squander time, for that is the stuff life is made of.

Benjamin Franklin

PM:

If a man loses pace with his companions, perhaps it is because he hears a different drummer. Let him step to the music in which he hears, however measured, or far away.

Henry David Thoreau

MAY 10

AM:

A man can get discouraged many times but he is not a failure until he begins to blame somebody else and stops trying.

John Burroughs

PM:

For though a righteous man falls seven times, he rises again...

Proverbs 24:16

MAY 11

AM:

All endeavor calls for the ability to tramp the last mile, shape the last plan, endure the last hours toil. The fight to the finish spirit is the one characteristic we must possess if we are to face the future as finishers.

Henry David Thoreau

PM:

When you get into a tight place and everything goes against you, till it seems as though you could not hang on a minute longer, never give up then, for it is just the place and time that the tide will turn.

Harriet Beecher Stowe

MAY 12

AM:

Applause waits on success.

Benjamin Franklin

PM:

When you start down the road of revenge, remember to dig two graves.

Chinese proverb

MAY 13

AM:

Sunshine is delicious, rain is refreshing, wind braces us up, snow is exhilarating; there is really no such thing as bad weather, only different kinds of good weather.

John Ruskin

PM:

Change is not made without inconvenience, even from worse to better.

Richard Hooker

MAY 14

AM:

Dignity consists not in possessing honors, but in the consciousness that we deserve them.

Aristotle

PM:

If I have eight hours to chop down a tree, I'd spend six hours sharpening an axe.

Abraham Lincoln

MAY 15

AM:

God gives talent, work transforms talent into genius.

Anna Pavlova

PM:

To the timid and hesitating everything is impossible because it seems so.

Walter Scott

MAY 16

AM:

You can't build a reputation on what you're going to do.

Henry Ford

PM:

The height of stupidity is doing the same thing over and over again, expecting different results.

Albert Einstein

MAY 17

AM:

Quality is not an act. It is a habit.

Aristotle

PM:

I have not failed. I have successfully discovered 1200 ideas that did not work.

Thomas Edison

MAY 18

AM:

Practical wisdom is only to be learned in the school of experience. Precepts and instruction are useful so far as they go, but, without the discipline of real life, they remain of the nature of theory only.

Samuel Smiles

PM:

Well done is better than well said.

Benjamin Franklin

MAY 19

AM:

Restlessness and discontent are the first necessities of progress.

Thomas Edison

PM:

Fear always springs from ignorance.

Ralph Waldo Emerson

MAY 20

AM:

Common sense is very uncommon.

Horace Greeley

PM:

When in doubt, don't.

Benjamin Franklin

MAY 21

AM:

To become what we are capable of becoming is the only end in life.

Robert Louis Stevenson

PM:

Everyone lives by selling something.

Robert Louis Stevenson

MAY 22

AM:

The first test of a truly great man is his humility. By humility I don't mean doubt of his powers or hesitation in speaking his opinion, but merely an understanding of the relationship of what he can say and what he can do.

John Ruskin

PM:

We have no more right to consume happiness without producing it than to consume wealth without producing it.

George Bernard Shaw

MAY 23

AM:

The vision that you glorify in your mind, the ideal that you enthrone in your heart - this you will build your life by, this you will become.

James Allen

PM:

The plans of the diligent lead to profit as surely as haste leads to poverty.

Proverbs 21:5

MAY 24

AM:

The highest reward for a man's toil is not what he gets for it but what he becomes by it.

John Ruskin

PM:

The apprenticeship of difficulty is one which the greatest of men have had to serve.

Samuel Smiles

MAY 25

AM:

Keep your fears to yourself but share your courage with others.

Robert Louis Stevenson

PM:

If they can see that you love them, you can say anything to them.

Richard Baxter

MAY 26

AM:

God helps them who help themselves.

Benjamin Franklin

PM:

There are three kinds of intelli-gence: one kind understands things for itself, the other appreciates what others can understand, the third understands neither for itself nor through others. This first kind is excellent, the second good, and the third kind useless.

Niccolo Machiavelli

MAY 27

AM:

Without a rich heart, wealth is an ugly beggar.

Ralph Waldo Emerson

PM:

High expectations are the key to everything.

Sam Walton

MAY 28

AM:

People do not lack strength; they lack will.

Victor Hugo

PM:

You are a poor specimen if you can't stand the pressure of adversity.

Proverbs 24:10

MAY 29

AM:

He who wishes to be obeyed must know how to command.

Niccolo Machiavelli

PM:

Energy and persistence conquer all things.

Benjamin Franklin

MAY 30

AM:

Our patience will achieve more than our force.

Edmund Burke

PM:

The greatest discovery of my generation is that human beings can alter their lives by altering their attitudes of mind.

William James

MAY 31

AM:

A man is as old as he feels himself to be.

English Proverb

PM:

In the long run, men hit only what they aim at. Therefore, they had better aim at something high.

Henry David Thoreau

JUNE

JUNE 1

AM:

Money speaks sense in a language all nations understand.

Aphra Behn

PM:

Lost wealth may be replaced by industry, lost knowledge by study, lost health by temperance or medicine, but lost time is gone forever.

Samuel Smiles

JUNE 2

AM:

Simplicity is the most difficult thing to secure in this world; it is the last limit of experience and the last effort of genius.

George Sand

PM:

The first one gets the oyster the second gets the shell.

Andrew Carnegie

JUNE 3

AM:

I have never been hurt by what I have not said.

Calvin Coolidge

PM:

Success in life is founded upon attention to the small things rather than to the large things; to the every day things nearest to us rather than to the things that are remote and uncommon.

Booker T. Washington

JUNE 4

AM:

Lost, yesterday, somewhere between sunrise and sunset, two golden hours, each set with sixty diamond minutes. No reward is offered for they are gone forever.

Horace Mann

PM:

The man who does not read good books has no advantage over the man who can't read them.

Mark Twain

JUNE 5

AM:

Men are not troubled by things themselves, but by their thoughts about them.

Epictectus

PM:

Faith is to believe what you do not yet see; the reward for this faith is to see what you believe.

St. Augustine

JUNE 6

AM:

Few people do business well who do nothing else.

Lord Chesterfield

PM:

There is hardly anything in the world that some man cannot make a little worse and sell a little cheaper, and the people who consider price only are this man's lawful prey.

John Ruskin

JUNE 7

AM:

It is what a man thinks of himself that really determines his fate.

Henry David Thoreau

PM:

The ability to convert ideas to things is the secret of outward success.

Henry Ward Beecher

JUNE 8

AM:

Most of the shadows of this life are caused by standing on one's own sunshine.

Ralph Waldo Emerson

PM:

He who is afraid of asking is ashamed of learning.

Danish proverb

JUNE 9

AM:

Deal with the faults of others as gently as your own.

Chinese proverb

PM:

A smooth sea never made a skilled mariner.

English Proverb

JUNE 10

AM:

He that lives upon hope will die fasting.

Benjamin Franklin

PM:

You must lose a fly to catch a trout.

George Herbert

JUNE 11

AM:

If you have no confidence in self, you are twice defeated in the race of life.

Marcus Garvey

PM:

Go as far as you can see; when you get there, you'll be able to see farther.

J.P. Morgan

JUNE 12

AM:

When a man is wrapped up in himself, he makes a pretty small package.

John Ruskin

PM:

A life of leisure and a life of laziness are two things. There will be sleeping enough in the grave.

Benjamin Franklin

JUNE 13

AM:

There is nothing like a dream to create the future.

Victor Hugo

PM:

The very first step toward success in any occupation is to become interested in it.

Dale Carnegie

JUNE 14

AM:

What you are speaks so loudly, I cannot hear what you are saying.

Ralph Waldo Emerson

PM:

The best day of your life is the one on which you decide your life is your own. No apologies or excuses; no one to lean on, rely on, or blame. The gift of life is yours - it is an amazing journey - and you alone are responsible for the quality of it.

Abraham Maslow

JUNE 15

AM:

The greatest mistake you can make in life is to be continually fearing you will make one.

Elbert Hubbard

PM:

In a start-up company, you basically throw out all assumptions every three weeks.

William Lyon Phelps

JUNE 16

AM:

Business is the salt of life.

Voltaire

PM:

You gain strength, courage and confidence by every experience in which you really stop to look fear in the face... You must do the thing which you think you cannot do.

Eleanor Roosevelt

JUNE 17

AM:

Excellence is to do a common thing in an uncommon way.

Booker T. Washington

PM:

What you get by achieving your goals is to as important as what you become by achieving your goals.

Henry David Thoreau

JUNE 18

AM:

Say not always what you know, but always know what you say.

Claudius

PM:

Boldness has genius, power, and magic in it. Begin it now.

Johann Wolfgang Von Goethe

JUNE 19

AM:

If I accept you as you are, I will make you worse; however, if I treat you though you are what you are capable of becoming, I help you become that.

Johann Wolfgang van Goethe

PM:

Common sense is in spite of, not as the result of education.

Victor Hugo

JUNE 20

AM:

The principal part of faith is patience.

George MacDonald

PM:

In business, three things are necessary: knowledge, temper, and time.

Owen Felltham

JUNE 21

AM:

Life is the art of drawing sufficient conclusions from insufficient premises.

Samuel Butler

PM:

He that waits upon fortune, is never sure of a dinner.

Benjamin Franklin

JUNE 22

AM:

Thought is the original source of all wealth, all success, all material gain, all great discoveries and inventions, and all achievement.

Claude M. Bristol

PM:

Experience is a dear teacher, but fools will learn at no other.

Benjamin Franklin

JUNE 23

AM:

Use what language you will, you can never say anything to others but what you are.

Ralph Waldo Emerson

PM:

Vision without action is a daydream. Action without vision is a nightmare.

Japanese Proverb

JUNE 24

AM:

To hold a man down, you have to stay down with him.

Booker T. Washington

PM:

Things are not difficult to make; what is difficult is putting ourselves in the state of mind to make them.

Constantin Brancusi

JUNE 25

AM:

If you once turn on your side after the hour at which you ought to rise, it is all over. Bolt up at once.

Walter Scott

PM:

Think of your own faults the first part of the night when you are awake and of the faults of others the latter part of the night when you are asleep.

Chinese proverb

JUNE 26

AM:

A lean compromise is better than a fat lawsuit.

George Herbert

PM:

No man's credit is as good as his money.

John Dewey

JUNE 27

AM:

A cheerful heart is good medicine, but a crushed spirit dries up the bones.

Proverbs 17:22

PM:

A constant struggle, a ceaseless battle to bring success from inhospitable surroundings, is the price of all great achievements.

Orison Swett Marden

JUNE 28

AM:

The secret of success is consistency of purpose.

Benjamin Disraeli

PM:

Worrying is like paying on a debt that may never come due.

Will Rogers

JUNE 29

AM:

Think like a man of action, act like a man of thought.

Henri Bergson

PM:

Take time to deliberate; but when the time for action arrives, stop thinking and go in.

Andrew Jackson

AM:

The magnificent and the ridiculous are so close that they touch.

Le Bovier de Fontenelle

PM:

One of the secrets of life is to keep our intellectual curiosity acute.

William Lyon Phelps

JULY

JULY 1

AM:

Do not worry if you have built your castles in the air. They are where they should be. Now put the foundations under them.

Henry David Thoreau

PM:

The devil's name is dullness.

Robert E. Lee

JULY 2

AM:

Great minds must be ready not only to take the opportunities, but to make them.

C.C. Colton

PM:

Fall seven times; stand up eight.

Japanese Proverb

JULY 3

AM:

It is almost as difficult to keep a first-class person in a fourth-class job, as it is to keep a fourth-class person in a first-class job.

Alexandre Dumas

PM:

Certainty? In this world nothing is certain but death and taxes.

Benjamin Franklin

JULY 4

AM:

Genius without education is like silver in the mine.

Benjamin Franklin

PM:

Success is dependent on effort.

Sophocles

JULY 5

AM:

Defeat is not the worst of failures. Not to have tried is the true failure.

George Edward Woodberry

PM:

The intensity of your desire governs the power with which the force is directed.

John McDonald

JULY 6

AM:

A man is rich in proportion to the number of things he can afford to let alone.

Henry David Thoreau

PM:

The only man who makes no mistakes is the man who never does anything.

Eleanor Roosevelt

JULY 7

AM:

God gives all birds their food but does not drop it into their nests.

Danish proverb

PM:

Faith consists in believing when it is beyond the power of reason to believe.

Voltaire

JULY 8

AM:

People will buy anything that is 'one to a customer.'

Sinclair Lewis

PM:

Only he is successful in his business who makes that pursuit which affords him the highest pleasure.

Henry David Thoreau

JULY 9

AM:

Show me a poorly uniformed troop and I'll show you a poorly uniformed leader.

Robert Baden-Powell

PM:

The greatest good we can do for others is not to share our riches with them, but to reveal their own.

Benjamin Disraeli

JULY 10

AM:

A good idea plus capable men cannot fail; it is better than money in the bank.

John Berry

PM:

To see far is one thing; going there is another.

Constantin Brancusi

JULY 11

AM:

Most people spend more time and energy going around problems than in trying to solve them.

Henry Ford

PM:

What is once well done is done forever.

Henry David Thoreau

JULY 12

AM:

The man who knows it can't be done counts the risk, not the reward.

Elbert Hubbard

PM:

Many men go fishing all of their lives without knowing that it is not fish they are after.

Henry David Thoreau

JULY 13

AM:

Be a Columbus to whole new continents and worlds within you, opening new channels, not of trade, but of thought.

Henry David Thoreau

PM:

Creditors have better memories than debtors.

Benjamin Franklin

JULY 14

AM:

Anybody can cut prices, but it takes brains to make a better article.

Philip Armour

PM:

Knowing what you can not do is more important than knowing what you can do. In fact, that's good taste.

A. C. Benson

JULY 15

AM:

Even if you are on the right track, you will get run over if you just sit there.

Will Rogers

PM:

The right thing to do never requires any subterfuge, it is always simple and direct.

Calvin Coolidge

JULY 16

AM:

A man thinks that by mouthing hard words he understands hard things.

Herman Melville

PM:

Capital isn't so important in business. Experience isn't so important. You can get both these things. What is important is ideas. If you have ideas, you have the main asset you need, and there isn't any limit to what you can do with your business and your life.

Harvey S. Firestone

JULY 17

AM:

Many of life's failures are people who did not realize how close they were to success when they gave up.

Thomas Edison

PM:

We should take care not to make the intellect our god; it has, of course, powerful muscles, but no personality.

Albert Einstein

JULY 18

AM:

Anyone who has begun to think, places some portion of the world in jeopardy.

John Dewey

PM:

One of the strongest characteristics of genius is the power of lighting its own fire.

John W. Foster

JULY 19

AM:

If nothing is to be done in the given situation, he must invent plausible reasons for doing nothing; and if something must be done, he must suggest the something. The unpardonable sin is to propose nothing, when action is imperative.

Charles Edward Merriam

PM:

If we will be quiet and ready enough, we shall find compensation in every disappointment.

Henry David Thoreau

JULY 20

AM:

Hope is the companion of power, and mother of success; for who so hopes strongly has within him the gift of miracles.

Samuel Smiles

PM:

The secret of success is to do the common things uncommonly well.

John D. Rockefeller

JULY 21

AM:

Nearly every man who develops an idea works it up to the point where it looks impossible, and then he gets discouraged. That's not the place to become discouraged.

Thomas Edison

PM:

Never interrupt someone doing what you said couldn't be done.

Amelia Earhart

JULY 22

AM:

Small opportunities are often the beginnings of great enterprises.

Demosthenes

PM:

You must not only aim right, but draw the bow with all your might.

Henry David Thoreau

JULY 23

AM:

The great accomplishments of man have resulted from the transmission of ideas and enthusiasm.

Thomas J. Watson

PM:

To succeed in business it is necessary to make others see things as you see them.

John H. Patterson

JULY 24

AM:

I believe fundamental honesty is the keystone of business.

Harvey S. Firestone

PM:

As is our confidence, so is our capacity.

William Hazlitt

JULY 25

AM:

You can't learn in school what the world is going to do next year.

Henry Ford

PM:

Perfection is achieved, not when there is nothing left to add, but when there is nothing left to take away.

Antoine de St. Exupery

JULY 26

AM:

That is happiness; to be dissolved into something complete and great.

Willa Cather

PM:

Realize what you really want. It stops you from chasing butterflies and puts you to work digging gold.

William Moulton Marston

JULY 27

AM:

The education of a man is never completed until he dies.

Robert E. Lee

PM:

The highest reward for a person's toil is not what he gets for it, but what he becomes by it.

John Ruskin

JULY 28

AM:

The only good luck many great men ever had was being born with the ability to overcome bad luck.

Channing Pollock

PM:

Knowledge conquered by labor becomes a possession - a property entirely our own.

Samuel Smiles

JULY 29

AM:

It takes many good deeds to build a good reputation, and only one bad one to lose it.

Benjamin Franklin

PM:

If one does not know to which port one is sailing, no wind is favorable.

Lucius Annaeus Seneca

JULY 30

AM:

Nothing is more difficult, and therefore more precious, than to be able to decide.

Napoleon Bonaparte

PM:

Hope is the struggle of the soul, breaking loose from what is perishable, and attesting her eternity.

Herman Melville

JULY 31

AM:

My great concern is not whether you have failed, but whether you are content with your failure.

Abraham Lincoln

PM:

Try not to become a man of success but rather to become a man of value.

Albert Einstein

AUGUST

AM:

In case of doubt, decide in favor of what is correct.

Karl Kraus

PM:

Storms make the oak grow deeper roots.

George Herbert

AUGUST 2

AM:

Life will always be to a large extent what we ourselves make it.

Samuel Smiles

PM:

When the character of a man is not clear to you, look at his friends (or business associates).

Japanese Proverb

AUGUST 3

AM:

Faith is not a thing which one "loses," we merely cease to shape our lives by it.

Georges Bernanos

PM:

You become a champion by fighting one more round. When things are tough, you fight one more round.

James J. Corbett

AUGUST 4

AM:

He who serves two masters has to lie to one.

Portuguese proverb

PM:

Words kill, words give life; they're either poison or fruit - you choose.

Proverbs 18:21

AUGUST 5

AM:

The next mile is only one a person really has to make.

Danish proverb

PM:

Things are not difficult to make; what is difficult is putting ourselves in the state of mind to make them.

Constantin Brancusi

AUGUST 6

AM:

All generalizations are dangerous, even this one.

Alexandre Dumas

PM:

What old people say you cannot do, you try and find that you can. Old deeds for old people, and new deeds for new.

Henry David Thoreau

AUGUST 7

AM:

An idea, to be suggestive, must come to the individual with the force of a revelation.

William James

PM:

A man cannot be comfortable without his own approval.

Mark Twain

AUGUST 8

AM:

When it is dark enough, you can see the stars.

Charles A Beard

PM:

The reason why so little is done, is generally because so little is attempted.

Samuel Smiles

AUGUST 9

AM:

There exist limitless opportunities in every industry. Where there is an open mind, there will always be a frontier.

Charles F. Kettering

PM:

The good man is the man who, no matter how morally unworthy he has been, is moving to become better.

John Dewey

AUGUST 10

AM:

The buyer needs a hundred eyes, the seller not one.

George Herbert

PM:

All the problems of the world could be settled easily if men were only willing to think. The trouble is that men very often resort to all sorts of devices in order not to think, because thinking is such hard work.

Thomas J. Watson

AUGUST 11

AM:

When a man has put a limit on what he will do, he has put a limit on what he can do.

Charles M. Schwab

PM:

If you stand up and be counted, from time to time you may get yourself knocked down. But remember this: A man flattened by an opponent can get up again. A man flattened by conformity stays down for good.

Thomas J. Watson

AUGUST 12

AM:

I am not disposed to complain that I have planted and others have gathered the fruits. A man has cause for regret only when he sows and no one reaps.

Charles Goodyear

PM:

Circumstances do not make the man, they reveal him.

James Allen

AUGUST 13

AM:

Take charge of your thoughts. You can do what you will with them.

Plato

PM:

Be pleasant until ten o'clock in the morning and the rest of the day will take care of itself.

Elbert Hubbard

AUGUST 14

AM:

There is no limit to what can be accomplished if it doesn't matter who gets the credit.

Ralph Waldo Emerson

PM:

The advertisements in a newspaper are more full knowledge in respect to what is going on in a state or community than the editorial columns are.

Henry Ward Beecher

AUGUST 15

AM:

Fame is a vapor, popularity an accident, and riches take wings. Only one thing endures and that is character.

Horace Greeley

PM:

Nothing so conclusively proves a man's ability to lead others as what he does from day to day to lead himself.

Thomas J. Watson

AUGUST 16

AM:

The only conquests which are permanent and leave no regrets are our conquests over ourselves.

Napoleon Bonaparte

PM:

Pleasant words are a honeycomb, sweet to the soul and healing to the bones.

Proverbs 16:24

AUGUST 17

AM:

In this world it is not what we take up, but what we give up, that makes us rich.

Henry Ward Beecher

PM:

To win without risk is to triumph without glory.

Pierre Corneille

AUGUST 18

AM:

Thinking is the hardest work there is, which is probably the reason why so few engage in it.

Henry Ford

PM:

For true success ask yourself these four questions: Why? Why not? Why not me? Why not now?

James Allen

AUGUST 19

AM:

It is not easy to be a pioneer - but oh, it is fascinating! I would not trade one moment, even the worst moment, for all the riches in the world.

Elizabeth Blackwell

PM:

Nothing great in the world has ever been accomplished without passion.

Georg Wilhelm Friedrich Hegel

AUGUST 20

AM:

Chance favors only the prepared mind.

Louis Pasteur

PM:

Don't be afraid to give up the good to go for the great.

John D. Rockefeller

AUGUST 21

AM:

Man is not the creature of circumstances. Circumstances are the creatures of men.

Benjamin Disraeli

PM:

There is no such thing as a great talent without great will power.

Honore de Balzac

AUGUST 22

AM:

If you want to truly understand something, try to change it.

Kurt Lewin

PM:

He that rises late must trot all day.

Benjamin Franklin

AUGUST 23

AM:

All growth depends upon activity. There is no development physically or intellectually without effort, and effort means work.

Calvin Coolidge

PM:

The law of harvest is to reap more than you sow. Sow an act, and you reap a habit. Sow a habit and you reap a character. Sow a character and you reap a destiny.

James Allen

AUGUST 24

AM:

Live your beliefs and you can turn the world around.

Henry David Thoreau

PM:

Don't find fault, find a remedy; anybody can complain.

Henry Ford

AUGUST 25

AM:

A friendship founded on business is better than a business founded on friendship.

John D. Rockefeller

PM:

Enthusiasm moves the world.

Arthur Balfour

AUGUST 26

AM:

History has demonstrated that the most notable winners usually encountered heartbreaking obstacles before they triumphed. They won because they refused to become discouraged by their defeats.

B. C. Forbes

PM:

Happiness is inward, and not outward; and so, it does not depend on what we have, but on what we are.

Henry van Dyke

AUGUST 27

AM:

The easiest way to riches is to get rid of some of your desires.

Petrarch

PM:

Great ambition is the passion of a great character. Those endowed with it may perform very good or very bad acts. All depends on the principles which direct them.

Napoleon Bonaparte

AUGUST 28

AM:

You must live in the present, launch yourself on every wave, find your eternity in each moment.

Henry David Thoreau

PM:

A person with a new idea is a crank until the idea succeeds.

Mark Twain

AUGUST 29

AM:

The mass of men lead lives of quiet desperation.

Henry David Thoreau

PM:

A person who doubts himself is like a man who would enlist in the ranks of his enemies and bear arms against himself. He makes his failure certain by himself being the first person to be convinced of it.

Alexandre Dumas

AUGUST 30

AM:

Do not hire a man who does your work for money, but him who does it for love of it.

Henry David Thoreau

PM:

Work as if you were to live a hundred years. Pray as if you were to die tomorrow.

Benjamin Franklin

AUGUST 31

AM:

Reason and judgment are the qualities of a leader.

Tacitus

PM:

Glory is fleeting, but obscurity is forever.

Napoleon Bonaparte

SEPTEMBER

SEPTEMBER 1

AM:

Success usually comes to those who are too busy to be looking for it.

Henry David Thoreau

PM:

Nothing in life is to be feared. It is only to be understood.

Marie Curie

SEPTEMBER 2

AM:

If you don't drive your business, you will be driven out of business.

B. C. Forbes

PM:

I have not failed. I've just found 10,000 ways that won't work.

Thomas Edison

SEPTEMBER 3

AM:

People who cannot find time for recreation are obliged sooner or later to find time for illness.

John Wanamaker

PM:

Success grants its rewards to the few, but is the dream of the multitude.

Dale Carnegie

SEPTEMBER 4

AM:

Only those who have patience to do simple things perfectly ever acquire the skill to do difficult things easily.

James J. Corbett

PM:

Every man is a damn fool for at least five minutes every day; wisdom consists in not exceeding the limit.

Elbert Hubbard

SEPTEMBER 5

AM:

The chief function of the body is to carry the brain around.

Thomas Edison

PM:

Our acts make or mar us, we are the children of our own deeds.

Victor Hugo

SEPTEMBER 6

AM:

A man always has two reasons for what he does - a good one, and the real one.

J. P. Morgan

PM:

You can speak well if your tongue can deliver the message of your heart.

John Ford

SEPTEMBER 7

AM:

Men are born to succeed, not to fail.

Henry David Thoreau

PM:

Faith is a passionate intuition.

William Wordsworth

SEPTEMBER 8

AM:

Four hostile newspapers are more to be feared than a thousand bayonets.

Napoleon Bonaparte

PM:

Initiative is doing the right thing without being told.

Victor Hugo

SEPTEMBER 9

AM:

If you believe everything you read, better not read.

Japanese Proverb

PM:

To survive, men and business and corporations must serve.

John H. Patterson

SEPTEMBER 10

AM:

To innovate is not to reform.

Edmund Burke

PM:

While we consider when to begin, it becomes too late.

Japanese Proverb

SEPTEMBER 11

AM:

If you would win a man to your cause, first convince him that you are his sincere friend.

Abraham Lincoln

PM:

There is a boundary to men's passions when they act from feelings; but none when they are under the influence of imagination.

Edmund Burke

SEPTEMBER 12

AM:

The big shots are only the little shots who keep shooting.

Christopher Morley

PM:

I do not believe a man can ever leave his business. He ought to think of it by day and dream of it by night.

Henry Ford

SEPTEMBER 13

AM:

There is far more opportunity than there is ability.

Thomas Edison

PM:

Once an organization loses its spirit of pioneering and rests on its early work, its progress stops.

Thomas J. Watson

SEPTEMBER 14

AM:

Men who are resolved to find a way for themselves will always find opportunities enough; and if they do not find them, they will make them.

Samuel Smiles

PM:

There's a way to do it better - find it.

Thomas Edison

SEPTEMBER 15

AM:

The reward of a thing well done is to have done it.

Ralph Waldo Emerson

PM:

A wise man will hear, and will increase learning; and a man of understanding shall attain unto wise counsels.

Proverbs 1:5

SEPTEMBER 16

AM:

If you have ideas, you have the main asset you need, and there isn't any limit to what you can do with your business and your life. Ideas are any man's greatest asset.

Harvey S. Firestone

PM:

Progress however, of the best kind, is comparatively slow. Great results cannot be achieved at once; and we must be satisfied to advance in life as we walk, step by step.

Samuel Smiles

SEPTEMBER 17

AM:

The darkest hour in any man's life is when he sits down to plan how to get money without earning it.

Horace Greeley

PM:

I feel sorry for the person who can't get genuinely excited about his work. Not only will he never be satisfied, but he will never achieve anything worthwhile.

Walter Chrysler

SEPTEMBER 18

AM:

Look and you will find it - what is unsought will go undetected.

Sophocles

PM:

Patience is a bitter plant, but it has sweet fruit.

German proverb

SEPTEMBER 19

AM:

Patience and Diligence, like faith, remove mountains.

William Penn

PM:

Live the life you've dreamed.

Henry David Thoreau

SEPTEMBER 20

AM:

A person can succeed at anything for which there is enthusiasm.

Charles M. Schwab

PM:

Ninety-nine percent of the failures come from people who have the habit of making excuses.

George Washington Carver

SEPTEMBER 21

AM:

The growth and development of people is the highest calling of leadership.

Harvey S. Firestone

PM:

If at first you don't succeed, try, try again. Then quit. There's no point in being a damn fool about it.

W. C. Fields

SEPTEMBER 22

AM:

Success is how high you bounce when you hit bottom.

George S. Patton

PM:

What lies behind us and what lies before us are small matters to what lies within us.

Ralph Waldo Emerson

SEPTEMBER 23

AM:

The world is moving so fast these days that the man who says it can't be done is generally interrupted by someone doing it.

Elbert Hubbard

PM:

The secret of my success is a two-word answer: Know people.

Harvey S. Firestone

SEPTEMBER 24

AM:

There is great force hidden in a gentle command.

George Herbert

PM:

There is no class so pitiably wretched as that which possesses money and nothing else.

Andrew Carnegie

SEPTEMBER 25

AM:

If I have the belief that I can do it, I shall surely acquire the capacity to do it even if I may not have it at the beginning.

Mahatma Gandhi

PM:

We are what we repeatedly do. Excellence, then, is not an act, but a habit.

Aristole

SEPTEMBER 26

AM:

Some men see things as they are and ask why. Others dream things that never were and ask why not.

George Bernard Shaw

PM:

Accept the challenges so that you can feel the exhilaration of victory.

George S. Patton

SEPTEMBER 27

AM:

Action speaks louder than words but not nearly as often.

Mark Twain

PM:

You cannot push anyone up the ladder unless he is willing to climb.

Andrew Carnegie

SEPTEMBER 28

AM:

The significant problems we face cannot be solved by the same level of thinking that created them.

Albert Einstein

PM:

If you don't think about the future, you won't have a future.

John Galsworthy

SEPTEMBER 29

AM:

It is hard for an empty bag to stand upright.

Benjamin Franklin

PM:

This is the only chance you will ever have on this earth with this exciting adventure called life. So why not plan it, and try to live it as richly and happily as possible?

Dale Carnegie

SEPTEMBER 30

AM:

Thought, not money, is the real business capital.

Harvey S. Firestone

PM:

Don't be afraid to give your best to what seemingly are small jobs. Every time you conquer one, it makes you that much stronger. If you do little jobs well, the big ones will tend to take care of themselves.

Dale Carnegie

OCTOBER

OCTOBER 1

AM:

When small men attempt great enterprises, they always end by reducing them to the level of their mediocrity.

Napoleon Bonaparte

PM:

Associate with men of good quality if you esteem your own reputation; for it is better to be alone than in bad company.

George Washington

OCTOBER 2

AM:

You can preach a better sermon with your life than with your lips.

Oliver Goldsmith

PM:

Make no small plans for they have no power to stir the soul.

Niccolo Machiavelli

OCTOBER 3

AM:

The greatest revolution of my life is the discovery that individuals can change the outer aspects of their lives by changing the inner attitudes of their minds.

William James

PM:

I have always been driven to buck the system, to innovate, to take things beyond where they've been.

Sam Walton

OCTOBER 4

AM:

Treat people as if they were what they ought to be, and you help them become what they are capable of being.

Johann Wolfgang von Goethe

PM:

Knowing is not enough, we must apply. Willing is not enough, we must do.

Johann Wolfgang van Goethe

OCTOBER 5

AM:

Life is too short to be small.

Benjamin Disraeli

PM:

Whenever an individual or a business decides that success has been attained, progress stops.

Thomas J. Watson

OCTOBER 6

AM:

People don't follow titles, they follow courage.

William Wells Brown

PM:

If you don't know where you are going, any road will get you there.

Lewis Carroll

OCTOBER 7

AM:

An executive is a person who always decides. Sometimes he decides correctly, but he always decides.

John H. Patterson

PM:

The very greatest things - great thoughts, discoveries, inventions - have usually been nurtured in hardship, often pondered over in sorrow, and at length established with difficulty.

Samuel Smiles

OCTOBER 8

AM:

Life is a series of experiences, each one of which makes us bigger, even though sometimes it is hard to realize this.

Henry Ford

PM:

Make no little plans; they have no magic to stir men's blood and probably will themselves not be realized. Make big plans; aim high in hope and work, remembering that a noble, logical diagram once recorded will not die.

Daniel Burnham

OCTOBER 9

AM:

Just for today I will exercise my soul in three ways: I will do somebody a good turn and not get found out. I will do at least two things I don't want to do.

William James

PM:

If one advances confidently in the direction of his dreams, and endeavors to live the life which he has imagined, he will meet with success unexpected in common hours.

Henry David Thoreau

OCTOBER 10

AM:

A little more persistence, a little more effort, and what seemed hopeless failure may turn to glorious success.

Elbert Hubbard

PM:

The rich rules over the poor, and the borrower is servant to the lender.

Proverbs 22:7

OCTOBER 11

AM:

If you don't say anything, you won't be called on to repeat it.

Calvin Coolidge

PM:

One machine can do the work of fifty ordinary men. No machine can do the work of one extraordinary man.

Elbert Hubbard

OCTOBER 12

AM:

Tell me and I'll forget; show me and I may remember; involve me and I'll understand.

Chinese Proverb

PM:

Nothing, not all the armies of the world, can stop an idea whose time has come.

Victor Hugo

OCTOBER 13

AM:

The way of the pioneer is always rough.

Harvey S. Firestone

PM:

You've got to get up every morning with determination if you're going to go to bed with satisfaction.

George Horace Lorimer

OCTOBER 14

AM:

Take time to deliberate, but when the time for action has arrived, stop thinking and go in.

Napoleon Bonaparte

PM:

It is nothing to die. It is frightful not to live.

Victor Hugo

OCTOBER 15

AM:

What impresses men is not mind, but the result of mind.

Walter Bagehot

PM:

When I am wrong, dear Lord, make me easy to change, and when I am right, make me easy to live with.

Peter Marshall

OCTOBER 16

AM:

To follow, without halt, one aim: that's the secret of success.

Anna Pavlova

PM:

The tragedy of life is not that man loses but that he almost wins.

Heywood Broun

OCTOBER 17

AM:

It is not enough to be busy. So are the ants. The question is: What are we busy about?

Henry David Thoreau

PM:

Make happy those who are near, and those who are far will come.

Chinese Proverb

OCTOBER 18

AM:

It takes a great man to be a good listener.

Calvin Coolidge

PM:

Nurture your mind with great thoughts; to believe in the heroic makes heroes.

Benjamin Disraeli

OCTOBER 19

AM:

Attitudes are more important than facts.

George MacDonald

PM:

You need to overcome the tug of people against you as you reach for high goals.

George S. Patton

OCTOBER 20

AM:

A man, as a general rule, owes very little to what he is born with - a man is what he makes of himself.

Alexander Graham Bell

PM:

To desire is to obtain; to aspire is to achieve.

James Allen

OCTOBER 21

AM:

No one could make a greater mistake than he who did nothing because he could do only a little.

Edmund Burke

PM:

He has achieved success who has worked well, laughed often, and loved much.

Elbert Hubbard

OCTOBER 22

AM:

In soloing - as in other activities - it is far easier to start something than it is to finish it.

Amelia Earhart

PM:

The best way to destroy an enemy is to make him a friend.

Abraham Lincoln

OCTOBER 23

AM:

Give to us, Lord, a clear vision that we may know where to stand and what to stand for - because unless we stand for something we shall fall for anything.

Peter Marshall

PM:

A failure is a man who has blundered, but is not able to cash in the experience.

Elbert Hubbard

OCTOBER 24

AM:

We are not human beings having a spiritual experience; we are spiritual beings having a human experience.

Pierre Teilhard de Chardin

PM:

Business? It's quite simple; it's other people's money.

Alexandre Dumas

OCTOBER 25

AM:

And while the law of competition may be sometimes hard for the individual, it is best for the race, because it ensures the survival of the fittest in every department.

Andrew Carnegie

PM:

Many people die at twenty-five and aren't buried until they are seventy-five.

Benjamin Franklin

OCTOBER 26

AM:

You get the best out of others when you get the best out of your-self.

Harvey S. Firestone

PM:

The man without a purpose is like a ship without a rudder - a waif, a nothing, a no-man. Have a purpose in life, and having it, throw strength of mind and muscle into your work as God has given you.

Thomas Carlyle

OCTOBER 27

AM:

And in the end it's not the years in your life that count. It's the life in your years.

Abraham Lincoln

PM:

Executive ability is deciding quickly and getting somebody else to do the work.

John G. Pollard

OCTOBER 28

AM:

No person was ever honored for what he received. Honor has been the reward for what he gave.

Calvin Coolidge

PM:

Experience is that marvelous thing that enable you to recognize a mistake when you make it again.

Franklin P. Jones

OCTOBER 29

AM:

The man who has received a benefit ought always to remember it, but he who has granted it ought to forget the fact at once.

Demosthenes

PM:

Victory belongs to the most persevering.

Napoleon Bonaparte

OCTOBER 30

AM:

The only fruitful promise of which the life of any individual or any nation can be possessed, is a promise determined by an ideal.

Herbert Croly

PM:

An investment in knowledge pays the best interest.

Benjamin Franklin

OCTOBER 31

AM:

It is a mistake to suppose that men succeed through success; they much oftener succeed through failures. Precept, study, advice, and example could never have taught them so well as failure has done.

Samuel Smiles

PM:

Most men lead lives of quiet desperation and go to the grave with the song still in them.

Henry David Thoreau

NOVEMBER

NOVEMBER 1

AM:

When you get something for nothing, you just haven't been billed for it yet.

Franklin P. Jones

PM:

Thought is a kind of opium; it can intoxicate us, while still broad awake; it can make transparent the mountains and everything that exists.

Henri Frederic Amiel

NOVEMBER 2

AM:

To avoid criticism, do nothing, say nothing, and be nothing.

Elbert Hubbard

PM:

Use soft words and hard arguments.

English Proverb

NOVEMBER 3

AM:

He who knows how to flatter also knows how to slander.

Napoleon Bonaparte

PM:

It's not what you pay a man, but what he costs you that counts.

Will Rogers

NOVEMBER 4

AM:

Genius is seldom recognized for what it is: a great capacity for hard work.

Henry Ford

PM:

To begin to think with purpose, is to enter the ranks of those strong ones who only recognize failure as one of the pathways to attainment.

James Allen

NOVEMBER 5

AM:

Every successful person I have heard of has done the best he could with the conditions as he found them, and not waited until next year for better.

Edgar Watson Howe

PM:

One of the chief reasons for success in life is the ability to maintain a daily interest in one's work, to have a chronic enthusiasm, to regard each day as important.

William Lyon Phelps

NOVEMBER 6

AM:

Never tell people how to do things. Tell them what to do and they will surprise you with their ingenuity.

George S. Patton

PM:

It isn't as important to buy as cheap as possible as it is to buy at the right time.

Jesse Livermore

NOVEMBER 7

AM:

Your best friend is he who brings out the best that is within you.

Henry Ford

PM:

Which form of proverb do you prefer Better late than never, or better never than late?

Lewis Carroll

NOVEMBER 8

AM:

Truth is in things, and not in words.

Herman Melville

PM:

If you don't drive your business, you will be driven out of business.

Henry Ford

NOVEMBER 9

AM:

Do your work with your whole heart, and you will succeed - there's so little competition.

Elbert Hubbard

PM:

If a man empties his purse into his head, no one can take it from him.

Bobby Knight

NOVEMBER 10

AM:

I never did anything by accident, nor did any of my inventions come by accident; they came by work.

Thomas Edison

PM:

Difficulties should act as a tonic. They should spur us to greater exertion.

B. C. Forbes

NOVEMBER 11

AM:

There are two times in a man's life when he should not speculate: when he can't afford it and when he can.

Mark Twain

PM:

No person was ever honored for what he received. Honor has been the reward for what he gave.

Calvin Coolidge

NOVEMBER 12

AM:

I recommend you to take care of the minutes, for the hours will take care of themselves.

Lord Chesterfield

PM:

A gem cannot be polished without friction, nor a man perfected without trials.

Lucius Annaeus Seneca

NOVEMBER 13

AM:

Nothing gives one person so much advantage over another as to remain cool and unruffled under all circumstances.

Thomas Jefferson

PM:

The highest reward that God gives us for good work is the ability to do better work.

Elbert Hubbard

NOVEMBER 14

AM:

A business is like an automobile, it has to be driven in order to get results.

B. C. Forbes

PM:

Action may not always bring happiness, but there is no happiness without action.

Benjamin Disraeli

NOVEMBER 15

AM:

A man is not paid for having a head and hands, but for using them.

Elbert Hubbard

PM:

Failure is simply the opportunity to begin again, this time more intelligently.

Henry Ford

NOVEMBER 16

AM:

No one is more miserable than the person who wills everything and can do nothing.

Claudius

PM:

Action speaks louder than words.

Dale Carnegie

NOVEMBER 17

AM:

It is energy - the central element of which is will - that produces the miracle that is enthusiasm in all ages. Everywhere it is what is called force of character and the sustaining power of all great action.

Samuel Smiles

PM:

Count what is in a man, not what is on him, if you would know what he is worth - whether rich or poor.

Henry Ward Beecher

NOVEMBER 18

AM:

If you want to be successful, it's just this simple. Know what you are doing. Love what you are doing. And believe in what you are doing.

Will Rogers

PM:

Worry is the interest paid by those who borrow trouble.

George Washington

NOVEMBER 19

AM:

An executive is a person who always decides sometimes he decides correctly, but he always decides.

John Henry Patterson

PM:

All mankind is divided into three classes: those that are immovable, those that are movable, and those that move.

Benjamin Franklin

NOVEMBER 20

AM:

We must not allow the clock and the calendar to blind us to the fact that each moment of life is a miracle and a mystery.

H.G. Wells

PM:

You cannot escape the responsibility of tomorrow by evading it today.

Abraham Lincoln

NOVEMBER 21

AM:

You must be the change you want to see in the world.

Mahatma Gandhi

PM:

The successful men of today are men of one overmastering idea, one unwavering aim, men of single and intense purpose.

Orison Swett Marden

NOVEMBER 22

AM:

Imagination is more important than knowledge.

Albert Einstein

PM:

To treat your facts with imagination is one thing, but to imagine your facts is another.

John Burroughs

NOVEMBER 23

AM:

We could hardly wait to get up in the morning.

Wilbur Wright

PM:

For a thing to remain undone, nothing more is needed than to think it done.

Baltasar Gracian

NOVEMBER 24

AM:

What lies behind us and what lies ahead of us are tiny matters compared to what lives within us.

Henry David Thoreau

PM:

Many a man's reputation would not know his character if they met on the street.

Elbert Hubbard

NOVEMBER 25

AM:

The miracle, or the power, that elevates the few is to be found in their perseverance under the promptings of a brave, determined spirit.

Mark Twain

PM:

To have done anything just for money is to have been truly idle.

Henry David Thoreau

NOVEMBER 26

AM:

Setting an example is not the main means of influencing another, it is the only means.

Albert Einstein

PM:

The world is wide, and I will not waste my life in friction when it could be turned into momentum.

Frances Willard

NOVEMBER 27

AM:

Before you try to convince anyone else, be sure you are convinced, and if you cannot convince yourself, drop the subject.

John Henry Patterson

PM:

All speech is vain and empty unless it be accompanied by action.

Demosthenes

NOVEMBER 28

AM:

There is no failure except in no longer trying.

Elbert Hubbard

PM:

You can't build a reputation on what you are going to do.

Henry Ford

NOVEMBER 29

AM:

We only think when we are con-fronted with problems.

John Dewey

PM:

Discipline is the soul of an army. It makes small numbers formi-dable, procures success to the weak, and esteem to all.

George Washington

NOVEMBER 30

AM:

If any man seeks for greatness, let him forget greatness and ask for truth, and he will find both.

Horace Mann

PM:

If advertisers spent the same amount of money on improving their products as they do on advertising, then they wouldn't have to advertise them.

Will Rogers

DECEMBER

AM:

Learn avidly. Question repeatedly what you have learned. Analyze it carefully. Then put what you have learned into practice intelligently.

Edward Cocker

PM:

To survive, men and business and corporations must serve.

John Henry Patterson

AM:

In all human affairs there are efforts, and there are results, and the strength of the effort is the measure of the result.

James Allen

PM:

If a man writes a better book, preaches a better sermon, or makes a better mousetrap than his neighbor, the world will make a beaten path to his door.

Ralph Waldo Emerson

DECEMBER 3

AM:

If a man writes a better book, preaches a better sermon, or makes a better mousetrap than his neighbor, the world will make a beaten path to his door.

Ralph Waldo Emerson

PM:

It isn't the big pleasures that count the most; it's making a great deal out of the little ones.

Jean Webster

DECEMBER 4

AM:

There is something that is much scarcer, something finer far, something rarer than ability. It is the ability to recognize ability.

Elbert Hubbard

PM:

It is one of the beautiful compensations of this life that no man sincerely tries to help another without helping himself.

Ralph Waldo Emerson

DECEMBER 5

AM:

Adversity makes men, and prosperity makes monsters.

Victor Hugo

PM:

Don't let yesterday use up too much of today.

Will Rogers

DECEMBER 6

AM:

A leader is a dealer in hope.

Napoleon Bonaparte

PM:

If one has not given everything, one has given nothing.

Georges Guynemer

DECEMBER 7

AM:

The intelligent man is always open to new ideas. In fact, he looks for them.

Proverbs 18:15

PM:

He who has a "why" to live for can bear almost any "how".

Friedrich Nietzsche

DECEMBER 8

AM:

Don't judge each day by the harvest you reap but by the seeds that you plant.

Robert Louis Stevenson

PM:

Success or failure in business is caused more by the mental attitude even than by mental capacities.

Walter Scott

DECEMBER 9

AM:

To talk much and arrive nowhere is the same as climbing a tree to catch a fish.

Chinese Proverb

PM:

Never give up, for that is just the place and time that the tide will turn.

Harriet Beecher Stowe

DECEMBER 10

AM:

For of sad words of tongue or pen, the saddest of these; it might have been.

John Greenleaf Whittier

PM:

Faith is an excitement and an enthusiasm: it is a condition of intellectual magnificence to which we must cling as to a treasure, and not squander on our way through life in the small coin of empty words, or in exact and priggish argument.

George Sand

DECEMBER 11

AM:

Outstanding leaders go out of their way to boost the self-esteem of their personnel. If people believe in themselves, it's amazing what they can accomplish.

Sam Walton

PM:

The real secret of success is enthusiasm.

Walter Chrysler

DECEMBER 12

AM:

It does not take much strength to do things, but it requires great strength to decide on what to do.

Elbert Hubbard

PM:

Next to excellence is the appreciation of it.

William Makepeace Thackeray

DECEMBER 13

AM:

I have made mistakes but I have never made the mistake of claiming that I have never made one.

James Gordon Bennett

PM:

People rarely succeed unless they have fun in what they are doing.

Dale Carnegie

DECEMBER 14

AM:

There is only one boss. The customer. And he can fire everybody in the company from the chairman on down, simply by spending his money somewhere else.

Sam Walton

PM:

Before anything else, preparation is the key to success.

Alexander Graham Bell

DECEMBER 15

AM:

No one ever gets far unless he accomplishes the impossible at least once a day.

Elbert Hubbard

PM:

If you want to achieve excellence, you can get there today. As of this second, quit doing less-than-excellent work.

Thomas J. Watson

DECEMBER 16

AM:

Theories are patterns without value. What counts is action.

Constantin Brancusi

PM:

It is easy to dodge our responsibilities, but we cannot dodge the consequences of dodging our responsibilities.

Josiah Stamp

DECEMBER 17

AM:

I cannot trust a man to control others who cannot control himself.

Robert E. Lee

PM:

Nothing great was ever achieved without enthusiasm.

Ralph Waldo Emerson

DECEMBER 18

AM:

The value of an idea lies in the using of it.

Thomas Edison

PM:

The surest way to reveal one's character is not through adversity, but by giving them power.

Abraham Lincoln

DECEMBER 19

AM:

Speak when you are angry, and you will make the best speech you will ever regret.

Ambrose Bierce

PM:

To enjoy enduring success, we should travel a little in advance of the world.

John McDonald

DECEMBER 20

AM:

A man has to learn that he cannot command things, but that he can command himself; that he cannot coerce the wills of others, but that he can mold and master his own will: and things serve him who serves Truth; people seek guidance of him who is master of himself.

James Allen

PM:

The mind is enriched by what it receives, the heart by what it gives.

Victor Hugo

DECEMBER 21

AM:

Imagination disposes of everything; it creates beauty, justice, and happiness, which is everything in the world.

Blaise Pascal

PM:

One is not born into the world to do everything, but to do something.

Henry David Thoreau

DECEMBER 22

AM:

Capital isn't scarce; vision is.

Sam Walton

PM:

I feel sorry for the person who can't get genuinely excited about his work. Not only will he never be satisfied, but he will never achieve anything worthwhile.

Walter Chrysler

DECEMBER 23

AM:

Get someone else to blow your horn and the sound will carry twice as far.

Will Rogers

PM:

Fear is the thought of admitted inferiority.

Elbert Hubbard

DECEMBER 24

AM:

A man never tells you anything until you contradict him.

George Bernard Shaw

PM:

What mankind wants is not talent; it is purpose.

Robert Bulwer-Lytton

DECEMBER 25

AM:

When you're thirsty it's too late to think about digging a well.

Japanese Proverb

PM:

He who walks with the wise grows wise.

Proverbs 13:20

DECEMBER 26

AM:

Few delights can equal the presence of one whom we trust utterly.

George MacDonald

PM:

Fortune befriends the bold.

John Dryden

DECEMBER 27

AM:

Our greatest glory is not in never failing, but in rising every time we fall.

Confucius

PM:

Take calculated risks. That is quite different from being rash.

George S. Patton

DECEMBER 28

AM:

It is better to be ignorant than mistaken.

Japanese Proverb

PM:

Sometimes the best deals are the ones we don't make.

William D. Brown

DECEMBER 29

AM:

I dream, therefore I exist.

August Strindberg

PM:

If a man has done his best, what else is there?

George S. Patton

DECEMBER 30

AM:

Quality means doing it right when no one is looking.

Henry Ford

PM:

The difference between perseverance and obstinacy is that one often comes from a strong will, and the other from a strong won't.

Henry Ward Beecher

DECEMBER 31

AM:

The most immutable barrier in nature is between one man's thoughts and another's.

William James

PM:

Keep up the old standards, and day by day raise them higher.

John Wanamaker